I0693258

Derechos Reservados

2023 © Juan M. Fernández Chico

2023 © After the Storm Editorial

Diseño de portada: Black Point Studio

Primera edición: Noviembre de 2023

© **The essential society: or when life matters
to what extent it is necessary.**
Esta obra está protegida por derechos de autor.
Queda prohibida su reproducción total o parcial,
física o impresa, para fines comerciales sin
autorización del autor o la editorial.

© **The essential society: or when life matters
to what extent it is necessary.**
This work is protected by copyright. It's total or
partial reproduction, physical or printed, for
commercial purposes without the author's or
publisher's authorization is prohibited.

-*-

Para más información sobre este y otros libros de
la editorial After the Storm, contactar
directamente en la página web

www.afterthestorm.store

AFTER THE STORM
EDITORIAL

FOREWORD

During the COVID-19 pandemic, many texts were written attempting to provide certainties about the phenomenon we were experiencing. Philosophers, scientists, writers, economists, political scientists, and a long list of well-known and not-so-well-known figures took the editorial stage with diverse writings and narratives. These ranged from the most intimate, heartbreaking, and unsettling to those attempting to find solutions to the social, political, and economic problems caused by the confinement—not the death of those who contracted the virus.

Preserving the lives of those in confinement was urgent, but not the care of the lives of those who, as Juan M. Fernández Chico says in this book, became dispensable (because they were necessary) to sustain the world economy. In this essential society, paradoxically, workers became highly substitutable—a twist, a provocation, as the author mentions in the epilogue of the text, offering another point of view of the pandemic. The essential society, therefore, became the invisible society for almost all of us who inhabited the confinement as a conditional mandate of the world order.

From the screens of our mobile devices, we observed the world as if it were a streaming miniseries that we could pause at any time to rest. A rest that the heroes of the pandemic did not have—the workers on the front line of health services, food production, and other essential services. This border had multiple dimensions, not only that of life and death but also of care, mainly that which would prevent the instrumental capitalist machinery from stopping.

"The Essential Society," by Juan M. Fernández Chico, is a written text that can be read in a flash, not only for its brevity but also for the careful administration of words that the author uses to recover the files from confinement and pandemic—phenomena of the 21st century that expose society's autoimmunity. Essential society, as Fernández

Chico proposes, is a timeless autoimmunity that reinvents itself from time to time, intending to extend the exceptionality of the world economy at particular moments in human history.

Roxana Rodríguez Ortiz
CDMX, December 6, 2023.

INTRODUCTION

A total lockdown policy was instituted globally during the deadliest peak of the COVID-19 pandemic. Leaving the house was an intrepid and almost deadly mission. However, amid the most severe health crisis of our generation, the world's governments accepted that life could not be put on pause, so they created exception zones for some jobs that risked their lives and to continue doing their jobs regularly to keep cities and countries afloat, creating an effect of bare life, in the words of Giorgio Agamben, a *homo sacer*, someone who is condemned to die but cannot be sacrificed, for those who had to go out every day, despite the danger involved in a virus about which little or nothing was known, other than that it was highly contagious and deadly. Here, I call that workforce The Essential Society, which represents those who perform vital but expendable work, whose life is reduced to the performance of a task to ensure that the lives of others can be kept as closely as possible to normal.

The decision to publish this relatively brief book arises from a compelling urgency to expedite the continuation of an ongoing dialogue. It was not the intention to delve into exhaustive detail but rather to initiate and sustain conversations that had already been initiated on various fronts. This book serves as an initial step in a broader discourse.

In essence, this work constitutes a personal endeavor to consider recent events, particularly those that unfolded rapidly and with profound consequences. The urgency to embark on this project was driven by a desire to capture the essence of a situation that, by its very nature, was bound to recur in the future. The events that transpired during the pandemic were not isolated incidents but reflective of broader trends and systemic issues that demand our collective attention.

The armies of dedicated individuals who comprise The Essential Society remain, to this day, grappling with the enduring ramifications of policies that were formulated and executed at the highest echelons of political and economic power. The consequences of decisions made in the corridors of authority have reverberated throughout the lives of those on the frontline, courageously fulfilling their essential roles. We must acknowledge and address these consequences as we strive for a more equitable and sustainable future. This book aims to be a part of that dialogue, illuminating the challenges faced by The Essential Society and fostering a deeper understanding of the intricacies at play in our society.

YOU BELONG TO OTHERS
EVEN IF YOU DON'T KNOW IT:

*[...] you may believe that your life
belongs to you, but it is false, it belongs to
those who love you, you belong to
Prudence, first of all, but also a little to
me, and maybe to other people I don't
know, but you belong to others even if you
don't know it.*

Anéantir, *Michel Houellebecq*

On March 19, 2020, when the
COVID-19 pandemic was on the rise in cases
and deaths, a bulletin was published on the
official website of the California government,
headed by Gavin Newsom, citing Executive
Order N -33-20. It required all California
residents to leave their homes under no
circumstances except when:

*[...] necessary to maintain the continuity
of operations of basic infrastructure
sectors and additional sectors that the
state public health official may designate
as essential to protect the health and well-*

*being of all Californians. (https://
covid19.ca.gov/es/essential-workforce/)*

I will analyze this document in more depth, as it is an almost foundational expression of the thinking behind creating a global essential workforce.

The bulletin listed a series of sectors and jobs classified as "Essential Workforce." Sectors such as medical care and public health, emergency, food, energy, water service, transportation, communications, technology, government, finance, industrial, commercial, and residential services, as well as defense bases.

A new list was expanded within each sector, explaining what work was considered essential.

That could be read as a desperate act by the governor to create a law expressly, which created a reasonably clear ditch that is impossible not to refer us to the most fundamental part of our humanity. When life is in imminent danger, the only thing that must remain is what is essential, like a body in a coma, which almost completely shuts down, leaving only the most vital organs and functions to keep that body alive.

California has accumulated more than 100,000 deaths from COVID-19 since the pandemic began, placing it at the top of the states with the most deaths, above Texas, with more than 90,000, and Florida, with just over 88 thousand.

That seemed quite obvious, even unquestionable. The sectors listed there were the minimum necessary to maintain as close to normality as possible. Any other non-essential sector or job listed there would have sounded frivolous and perverse—for example, a bag store, a spa, or a casino.

However, even with that, we cannot help but ask: essential, for whom?

For those who had to carry out the essential jobs, no. They would be in an intermediate, uncertain place, floating between life and death. It is impossible not to think about the bare life by Giorgio Agamben: workers who were condemned to carry the machinery of neighborhoods, cities, and countries. At the same time, some of us stayed locked in our homes. Their lives were almost seen as a sacrifice, a holocaust in the strictest definition of the word. Thrown into the streets, while a violent and unknown virus moved silently, putting all nations in check without exceptions. They were launched to turn on and operate machines that could not stop.

Is the essential society really essential, or is it a discursive construction that only changes the name of those labor sectors that make up the vital structure of our society, mainly capital, using a name that is a sanitized tautology?

My reading goes precisely that way.

The essential society is the reflection of our social history. For some of us to live in peace and comfort, we must make sacrifices that allow our lifestyle to function normally. These sacrifices tend to be the most precarious and marginalized links, especially in the world of work, while the wealthiest sectors set normality. Therefore, the pandemic did not create the essential society; it only made it more evident, choosing an almost heroic word to name what was unnamed. It was no longer necessary to generate argumentative or nominative devices to create a title to what we dare not to name, to accept that there are expendable and sacrificial lives, which are as essential as they are replaceable.

EXECUTIVE ORDER N-33-20: A PLAY WITH BIOPOWER, SOVEREIGNTY, AND GOVERNANCE IN TIMES OF CRISIS

I take this executive order, as well as the bulletin that laid the foundations for forming an essential workforce to keep public infrastructure running, as an example of the thinking that permeated all governments and health institutions worldwide, using some concepts and techniques from Michel Foucault's discourse analysis, as it is a handy toolbox to reveal the forces that move behind the words.

Michel Foucault's discourse analysis can provide insights into the language, power dynamics, and underlying ideologies embedded behind this document. Foucault's concepts, such as governmentality, biopower, and the relationship between sovereignty and governance, offer a lens through which we can go deeply into what is behind the conformation of an essential workforce.

Let's take a look at the first Executive Order and how the document is organized.

EXECUTIVE DEPARTMENT
STATE OF CALIFORNIA

EXECUTIVE ORDER N-33-20

WHEREAS on March 4, 2020, I proclaimed a State of Emergency to exist in California as a result of the threat of COVID-19; and

WHEREAS in a short period of time, COVID-19 has rapidly spread throughout California, necessitating updated and more stringent guidance from federal, state, and local public health officials; and

WHEREAS for the preservation of public health and safety throughout the entire State of California, I find it necessary for all Californians to heed the State public health directives from the Department of Public Health.

NOW, THEREFORE, I, GAVIN NEWSOM, Governor of the State of California, in accordance with the authority vested in me by the State Constitution and statutes of the State of California, and in particular, Government Code sections 8567, 8627, and 8665 do hereby issue the following Order to become effective immediately:

IT IS HEREBY ORDERED THAT:

1) To preserve the public health and safety, and to ensure the healthcare delivery system is capable of serving all, and prioritizing those at the highest risk and vulnerability, all residents are directed to immediately heed the current State public health directives, which I ordered the Department of Public Health to develop for the current statewide status of COVID-19. Those directives are consistent with the March 19, 2020, Memorandum on Identification of Essential Critical Infrastructure Workers During COVID-19 Response, found at: https://covid19.ca.gov/. Those directives follow:

ORDER OF THE STATE PUBLIC HEALTH OFFICER
March 19, 2020

To protect public health, I as State Public Health Officer and Director of the California Department of Public Health order all individuals living in the State of California to stay home or at their place of residence except as needed to maintain continuity of operations of the federal critical infrastructure sectors, as outlined at https://www.cisa.gov/identifying-critical-infrastructure-during-covid-19. In addition, and in consultation with the Director of the Governor's Office of Emergency Services, I may designate additional sectors as critical in order to protect the health and well-being of all Californians.

Pursuant to the authority under the Health and Safety Code 120125, 120140, 131080, 120130(c), 120135, 120145, 120175 and 120150, this order is to go into effect immediately and shall stay in effect until further notice.

The federal government has identified 16 critical infrastructure sectors whose assets, systems, and networks, whether physical or virtual, are considered so vital to the United States that their incapacitation or destruction would have a debilitating effect on security, economic security, public health or safety, or any combination thereof. I order that Californians working in these 16 critical infrastructure sectors may continue their work because of the importance of these sectors to Californians' health and well-being.

This Order is being issued to protect the public health of Californians. The California Department of Public Health looks to establish consistency across the state in order to ensure that we mitigate the impact of COVID-19. Our goal is simple, we want to bend the curve, and disrupt the spread of the virus.

The supply chain must continue, and Californians must have access to such necessities as food, prescriptions, and health care. When people need to leave their homes or places of residence, whether to obtain or perform the functions above, or to otherwise facilitate authorized necessary activities, they should at all times practice social distancing.

2) The healthcare delivery system shall prioritize services to serving those who are the sickest and shall prioritize resources, including personal protective equipment, for the providers providing direct care to them.

3) The Office of Emergency Services is directed to take necessary steps to ensure compliance with this Order.

4) This Order shall be enforceable pursuant to California law, including, but not limited to, Government Code section 8665.

IT IS FURTHER ORDERED that as soon as hereafter possible, this Order be filed in the Office of the Secretary of State and that widespread publicity and notice be given of this Order.

This Order is not intended to, and does not, create any rights or benefits, substantive or procedural, enforceable at law or in equity, against the State of California, its agencies, departments, entities, officers, employees, or any other person.

IN WITNESS WHEREOF I have hereunto set my hand and caused the Great Seal of the State of California to be affixed this 19th day of March 2020.

GAVIN NEWSOM
Governor of California

ATTEST:

ALEX PADILLA
Secretary of State

The document begins by invoking a state of emergency due to the COVID-19 threat. This proclamation immediately sets the stage for a discourse of urgency and crisis, a typical strategy to legitimize exceptional measures.

Governor Newsom directs Californians to heed State public health directives developed by the Department of Public Health. The reference to "public health" aligns with the biopolitical discourse discussed by Foucault, where power operates through managing populations' health.

The document identifies "essential critical infrastructure workers" following a March 19, 2020 Memorandum. This designation reflects the concept of the Essential Society, a concept brought into focus by the COVID-19 pandemic. Certain workers are labeled as indispensable to the functioning of society, mirroring Agamben's homo sacer, who can be killed but not sacrificed, and embodying the fragile balance between life and death.

The Governor's decision to label certain workers as essential echoes the sovereign power discussed by Giorgio Agamben, who decides on the state of exception and who is included or excluded from legal rights and protections. This decision-making process becomes central to defining life's political relevance.

Throughout the document, there is a recurring emphasis on protecting public health, reflecting a biopolitical approach, where power is exercised for the health and well-being of the population. Foucault's concepts of biopower and governmentality come into play as the state assumes the role of regulating life to ensure its continuation.

The executive order highlights the prioritization of healthcare services for the sickest, reflecting the distribution of resources in a manner reminiscent of Agamben's focus on the role of sovereign power in making decisions about life and death.

The document underscores the enforceability of the order, demonstrating the exercise of sovereign power. It also speaks to the state's capacity to maintain order and discipline through regulatory mechanisms, concepts explored by both Foucault and Agamben.

The order explicitly states that it does not create substantive or procedural rights enforceable at law, emphasizing the exceptional nature of the measures taken. This echoes Foucault's idea of exceptional laws and Agamben's discussion of the state of exception.

Governmentality and Biopower

This executive order, issued by California's Governor Gavin Newsom, reflects elements of Foucault's concept of governmentality. It signifies the State's exercise of authority in a time of crisis. The order is rooted in the government's desire to protect its citizens' public health and safety. It is a form of biopower—a form of governance that controls and regulates the health and well-being of populations. In this context, the State's response to COVID-19 is not merely a matter of maintaining law and order but involves the management and regulation of the health and lives of its citizens, deciding who lives and who does not.

Sovereignty and Governance

The order highlights the intersection of sovereignty and governance. While sovereignty traditionally entails the power to decide about life and death, this executive order demonstrates how the State, through its regulatory authority, controls citizens' lives differently. It emphasizes the ability to decide who is included and excluded from certain rights and protections, aligning with Foucault's notion of the biopolitical power of the State.

Subjectification

Foucault's concept of subjectification can be observed in the document as it calls upon all residents to heed the State's directives. This demonstrates how individuals are expected to subject themselves to the authority of the State, particularly in times of crisis, highlighting the power dynamics between the State and its citizens.

The Role of Essential Workers

The document refers to the federal government's identification of 16 critical infrastructure sectors. This references a system of categorizing and controlling workers based on the importance of their roles, a reflection of biopolitical governance. The essential workers are identified as those who may continue their work during the crisis, showcasing how the State defines and prioritizes specific employment categories in the interest of public health and safety.

Exception and Normalization

The executive order suspends specific standard rules and regulations, making exceptions to enforcing new measures in response to the crisis. This reflects Foucault's idea of how power operates in exceptional circumstances, leading to the establishment of new norms and controls.

The analysis of Executive Order N-33-20 exemplifies how governmental power is exercised during a state of emergency, significantly impacting the lives and actions of the population. It underscores the intricate power dynamics, biopolitical governance, and the exercise of sovereignty that come into play in the context of the COVID-19 pandemic response in California.

GLOBAL CONTEXT
THE COVID-19 PANDEMIC AND
THE GLOBAL HANDBRAKE

The outbreak of COVID-19 in Wuhan, China, in December 2019 signaled the onset of an unprecedented global health crisis. As the virus swiftly traversed international borders, governments worldwide were compelled to respond with various measures to contain and safeguard their populations. These measures encompassed lockdowns, travel restrictions, business closures, and, notably, the identification of essential sectors and occupations.

An illustrative example of the urgency with which political leaders reacted to this crisis can be seen in Executive Order N-33-20, issued by the California government in March 2020. This directive swiftly established a list of essential jobs deemed crucial for maintaining the functioning of society amid the emergent crisis. However, the designation of essential roles raised profound questions regarding who had the authority to define the essentiality of a job and, more crucially, for whom it was genuinely essential.

Through analyzing speeches and statements made by political leaders worldwide, this book explores the construction and justification of the concept of The Essential Society. It endeavors to scrutinize whether this categorization was merely a reactive response to the urgency of the pandemic or whether it reveals a more profound logic deeply entrenched within the bedrock of our social and economic structures. This analysis will also explore how this notion of essentiality influenced the recognition, gratitude, working conditions, and protection afforded to those considered essential workers.

Throughout the pages of this book, we will argue that The Essential Society is not a creation of the COVID-19 pandemic but rather a reflection of our enduring social and economic history. It mirrors a society where specific precarious and marginalized sectors are burdened with the responsibility of upholding the vital machinery of society to ensure the well-being of other, often more privileged, segments.

In its ferocious and unrelenting grip, the pandemic did not invent The Essential Society, but it undoubtedly made its existence more glaringly evident. It exposed the profound fragility embedded in our social structure, particularly in moments of crisis, laying bare the intricate interplay between social hierarchies, economic dynamics, and the resilience of the human spirit. In a global context, The Essential Society became a microcosm of societal inequalities, a stark reminder of the structural imbalances that persisted even as the world grappled with a familiar foe.

THE CONSTRUCTION OF THE ESSENTIAL SOCIETY.

In this section, I want to take a quick tour of some of the speeches or announcements of the most prominent global leaders during the pandemic. It is not an exhaustive list; there is no selection criterion other than taking the most prominent political representatives worldwide.

I am not doing a deep, detailed, or methodical analysis, neither in its choice of the extensive possible corpus, the fragment selection, nor in the interpretation.

In this section, I seek to create a song from the orchestra of different voices but synchronized in the same thought about combatting the virus, but without slowing down global economies and infrastructures.

During the COVID-19 pandemic, world leaders from different countries issued speeches and statements in recognition of the importance of the essential workforce. Below, I will analyze some of these fragments to understand how the work of employees considered essential was perceived and valued during this critical period.

1. "The essential workforce is the backbone of our society and deserves our deepest gratitude for their dedication and bravery during difficult times." - Angela Merkel, Chancellor of Germany.

Angela Merkel's comment highlights the crucial relevance of essential workers to the functioning of society. The recognition of their dedication and bravery reflects the understanding that these employees faced risk and exposure to the virus while carrying out their essential duties.

2. "Our essential workers are on the front lines of the battle against this pandemic. Their commitment and sacrifice are essential to keeping our community safe, and we must honor them." - Justin Trudeau, Prime Minister of Canada.

Justin Trudeau emphasizes the bravery and commitment of essential workers by placing them on the "front lines" against COVID-19. This recognition seeks to highlight these employees' crucial role in the protection and well-being of the community, which in turn makes them deserving of honor and recognition.

3. "Key workers are unsung heroes who risk their lives to keep the essential services we need to survive running. We must always support and protect them." - Jacinda Ardern, Prime Minister of New Zealand.

Jacinda Ardern's statement highlights the selflessness and sacrifice of essential workers, describing them as "unsung heroes." This characterization underscores the hard work and risks these employees faced as they continued their vital work. Likewise, her call to support and protect them highlights the need to provide adequate support during the crisis.

4. "The pandemic has made clear the importance of essential workers. They are the

ones who supply us, care for us, and keep us connected. We must recognize their work and ensure they are protected." - Tedros Adhanom Ghebreyesus, Director General of the World Health Organization.

Tedros Adhanom Ghebreyesus' commentary emphasizes the multifaceted role of essential workers, who were critical in supplying, caring for, and connecting communities during the pandemic. Their call to recognize their work and ensure their protection underscores the need to ensure their well-being as they face the crisis.

These speech excerpts show how world leaders recognized and valued the work of the essential workforce during the COVID-19 pandemic. The rhetoric employed by these leaders sought to highlight the bravery, commitment, and dedication of essential workers while underscoring their crucial role in the functioning and well-being of society in times of crisis.

CAPITALISM AND THE HIERARCHIZATION OF LIFE

The Essential Society is a stark illustration of the profound impact of capitalism on our societal structures. As an economic and social system, capitalism is built to maximize profits within a competitive environment. This pursuit often leads to the exploitation and marginalization of specific labor sectors in the relentless quest for economic efficiency.

The COVID-19 pandemic laid bare the contradictions and vulnerabilities inherent in this capitalist framework. It revealed a paradox: those who sustained the very foundation of society during its most critical hours were the same individuals who had long endured job insecurity, low wages, and unfavorable working conditions. During the crisis, essential workers became momentary heroes, lauded for their sacrifices, courage, and dedication. However, once the immediate threat subsided, many were left to confront the harsh reality of their poorly compensated work and suboptimal employment conditions.

This juxtaposition underscores the inherent hierarchization of life within a capitalist system. The essential roles crucial for society's survival are often undervalued, underpaid, and unprotected. The pandemic spotlighted how specific labor sectors, despite their indispensability, were routinely marginalized and excluded from the benefits and security that should accompany such vital roles.

It became evident that the capitalist logic had, over time, deepened the chasm between the privileged and the marginalized. The pandemic merely served as a magnifying glass, exposing these longstanding inequalities. It demonstrated that a society driven by profit and competition can unintentionally perpetuate a two-tiered system, where some lives are accorded significantly more value and protection than others.

As we reflect on the experiences of The Essential Society, it becomes clear that the pandemic presents an opportunity to reassess the values and principles that underpin our societal structures. It urges us to consider whether the hierarchization of life inherent in capitalism aligns with our collective moral compass and principles of justice.

The Essential Society's contribution to our daily lives is immeasurable, and their well-being and security should not be mere afterthoughts. Addressing the inequities exposed by the pandemic requires a fundamental reconsideration of how we value and remunerate essential work, how we provide job security and fair wages, and how we construct a society where the dignity and worth of each individual, regardless of their occupation, are honored. It is a call to revisit capitalism's very essence and ensure that it serves the interests of the many rather than the few, respecting the dignity of every person who contributes to the essential functioning of our society.

HOMO SACER: THE SOVEREIGN, BARE LIFE, AND THE ESSENTIAL SOCIETY

This chapter delves into the intricate concepts of *homo sacer*, sovereignty, and bare life, as articulated by Giorgio Agamben. These concepts, deeply rooted in political philosophy, play a significant role in shaping our understanding of the Essential Society, especially in the context of the COVID-19 pandemic. By examining Agamben's writings and insights, we aim to illuminate the interplay between these ideas and their connection to the broader implications for governance and societal ethics.

Agamben's exploration of sovereignty offers a profound paradox: the sovereign exists outside and inside the juridical order. The sovereign possesses the power to create laws, declare a state of exception, and decide who wields authority. Simultaneously, the sovereign remains an integral part of the order they navigate. This paradoxical positioning exposes the tension between sovereignty and the juridical order, where the sovereign becomes the figure who defines the frame of life.

According to Agamben, every general rule necessitates a homogenous medium, a regular, everyday frame of life to which it can be applied. The rule relies on a recognizable context, a structured framework that establishes a sense of normality and order. The sovereign, however, retains the power to decide this frame of life, determining what aspects should be maintained and what constitutes the exception. The exception, as Agamben suggests, brings to light the intricacies of the general more vividly than the general itself. This emphasis on the exception as a structure of sovereignty highlights the intimate relationship between sovereign power and bare life.

Bare life, often understood as life stripped down to its biological existence, is the foundation of Agamben's exploration. It represents existence devoid of the rights, legal protections, and social constructs that typically accompany human life. Bare life is society's most vulnerable and marginalized stratum, living within the precarious space between inclusion and exclusion. The sovereign, who decides the state of exception and frames the general, wields power over this bare life.

Agamben's writings evoke chilling images of individuals who have been reduced to the status of homo sacer, figures who can be killed with impunity but cannot be sacrificed in a ritualistic sense. The COVID-19 pandemic transformed essential workers into contemporary homo sacer, individuals celebrated as heroes for their vital roles in society and rendered as sacrificial pawns to maintain a semblance of normality.

The concepts of *homo sacer*, sovereignty, and bare life offer a powerful lens through which we can examine the Essential Society during the COVID-19 pandemic. Agamben's insights highlight the tensions between governance and the vulnerability of those existing in states of exception. These themes are fundamental in understanding how the pandemic exposed the precarious nature of essential workers and the broader implications for ethical governance and societal justice.

THE ESSENTIAL SOCIETY, BARE LIFE, AND SOVEREIGN POWER: UNVEILING THE PANDEMIC PARADOX

The COVID-19 pandemic brought about a seismic shift in how we perceive the Essential Society, illuminating the complexities underlying its formation and operation. This chapter delves into the intricate relationship between the Essential Society, the concept of Bare Life, and the exercise of sovereign power. Through a comprehensive examination, we explore how these elements intersected during the pandemic and their profound implications for our understanding of governance, ethics, and social justice.

The Essential Society and the Bare Life

The Essential Society, a product of governmental urgency and desperation, took center stage in response to the pandemic's dire circumstances. Its inception resulted from the need to identify indispensable sectors and roles, even in a global health crisis. Sectors such as medical care, emergency services, food production, and transportation were thrust into the spotlight as fundamental pillars sustaining the population's well-being.

However, lurking beneath this response lay a fundamental question: Who comprises this Essential Society? To unravel this question, we turn to the profound concept of "bare life." This ancient notion, reinterpreted by contemporary philosophers and thinkers, involves life reduced to its bare biological existence. Stripped of the layers of rights, legal protections, and social constructs that typically accompany human existence, bare life embodies society's most vulnerable and marginalized segment.

The pandemic cast essential workers as modern-day homo sacer, a term initially explored by Italian philosopher Giorgio Agamben. Homo sacer signifies individuals who can be killed with impunity but cannot be sacrificed in a ritualistic or religious sense. In our contemporary crisis, it represents those who led precarious lives, fully exposed to the virus's perils while diligently fulfilling their job responsibilities. These individuals became heroes celebrated for their valor but were also rendered as sacrificial pawns in the pursuit of societal normality.

This chapter unravels the paradoxical nature of the Essential Society. It symbolizes a duality of life and death, normality and uncertainty. Essential workers embodied bravery and vulnerability, carrying the emotional weight of society's hopes and fears. Their recognition and inclusion in governmental discourse aimed to provide certainty amid uncertainty and revealed existing structural inequalities in society. The Essential Society mirrors the intricate interplay between societal functioning and the working and social conditions of those sustaining it.

Sovereign Violence and the Exclusion of Bare Life

Sovereign power, often regarded as the pinnacle expression of the state's authority, rests upon the exclusion of "bare life." At its core, sovereignty entails the state's prerogative to decide matters of life and death and determine who is encompassed by legal rights and protections and who remains vulnerable and excluded.

The exclusion of "bare life" finds embodiment in the concept of "homo sacer," an individual who can be killed without the act being considered a ritualistic or religious sacrifice. This exclusion forms the cornerstone upon which the political dimension is constructed, ultimately giving rise to the foundation of sovereign power.

During the COVID-19 pandemic, we witnessed sovereign violence against "bare life." Essential workers, the courageous individuals on the front lines of the battle against the virus, became potential victims of exposure to contagion. Their essential roles placed them in a precarious position, with their lives subject to the decisions of sovereign power. This power determined their inclusion in the Essential Society and, by extension, their access to protection.

The pandemic starkly reminds us of how sovereign power can be inadvertently wielded as a weapon against the most vulnerable in society. Essential workers celebrated as heroes for their indispensable roles also found themselves at the mercy of sovereign authority. This chapter leads us to contemplate the extent to which the state should exercise its authority over life and death and whether our societal structures should be reimagined to provide equitable protections and rights for all, irrespective of occupation or social status.

In unifying the themes of the Essential Society, Bare Life, and sovereign power, we uncover the multi-faceted challenges that emerged during the COVID-19 pandemic. This chapter underscores the importance of revisiting and reevaluating the fundamental principles of governance, with a keen focus on justice, equity, and the protection of all members of society, irrespective of their role or status. The pandemic prompts us to question the ethical implications of sovereign power and its role in shaping the destinies of those existing in the state of "bare life." These interconnected themes serve as a cornerstone for understanding the intricate dynamics of the pandemic and its broader societal impact.

THEORETICAL AND CONCEPTUAL FRAMEWORK: THE FLOATING SIGNIFIER IN THE CONTEXT OF ESSENTIAL SOCIETY

The concept of a floating signifier is a pivotal notion within psychoanalysis, semiotics, and poststructuralist theory. It finds resonance in the discussion of the "essential society" that emerged during the COVID-19 pandemic, with insights drawn from the works of Jacques Lacan and Ernesto Laclau.

In essence, a floating signifier is a sign or symbol that lacks a fixed, stable, or predetermined meaning. It is detached from a specific and unchanging signified, allowing it to be open to a multitude of interpretations and emotional resonances. This detachment from a singular, fixed meaning offers the floating signifier a degree of ambiguity and polysemy, making it a powerful tool for constructing meaning and identity.

Jacques Lacan's psychoanalytic theories are instrumental in understanding the concept of the floating signifier. Lacan's work on the signifier-signified relationship and the inherent instability of language underscores how signifiers can acquire a multiplicity of meanings based on an individual's psychic and emotional constitution. In Lacanian terms, the floating signifier represents the perpetual deferral of meaning and highlights the role of the unconscious in shaping our interpretations.

Ernesto Laclau, a key figure in poststructuralist political theory, further expands on the notion of the floating signifier within political discourse. Laclau argues that political identities and movements often rely on constructing empty signifiers whose content is not fixed but relatively open to constant articulation and re-articulation. These empty signifiers serve as nodal points around which political discourse coalesces.

The "essential society" during the COVID-19 pandemic serves as a compelling case study for the concept of the floating signifier. This societal construct lacks a fixed and universally agreed-upon meaning. Instead, it acquires meaning through a complex interplay of fears, hopes, and individual interpretations. The "essential society" represents a signifier detached from a singular, stable signified.

On the one hand, essential workers are perceived as heroes, embodying the hope of safeguarding life and maintaining a semblance of normality in the face of crisis. They become symbols of life and resilience, signifying security and stability. This interpretation aligns with Lacan's concept of signifiers acquiring a range of emotional resonances.

Conversely, the essential activity immerses these workers in a darker, risk-laden reality, intertwining their roles with notions of death and imminent danger. Here, the same signifier signifies vulnerability and risk, resonating with Lacan's assertion that signifiers can evoke various emotional and psychological responses.

Governments' categorization of "essential workers" further underscores the floating signifier nature of the "essential society." Governments aim to provide a semblance of certainty and control by designating and listing essential sectors and jobs, yet these designations remain open to interpretation. Despite their crucial role, essential workers often find themselves in precarious and marginalized working conditions, highlighting the ambiguity of their categorization and the tensions surrounding their value and recognition.

The "essential society" epitomizes the concept of a floating signifier. It symbolizes a duality of meaning—life and death, normality and uncertainty. The emotional and psychological weight of essential workers is emblematic of the ever-shifting interpretations ascribed to such signifiers. The categorization's inherent tensions also underline the concept's fluidity and open-endedness. The "essential society" is a contemporary illustration of how floating signifiers shape identity, meaning, and social discourse in times of crisis.

Towards a floating signifier

The constitution of the essential society during the COVID-19 pandemic emerged as an empty or floating signifier in the collective consciousness of society. This notion was formed through a complex intersection of fears and hopes, giving an ambiguous and ambivalent meaning to the work activities and roles played by doctors, transporters, constructors, and service providers who continued working amid the crisis to maintain operations of the society.

Essential workers considered the backbone of society in times of uncertainty and challenges, assumed a paradigmatic duality in public perception. On the one hand, they were seen as heroes who bravely faced a high-risk situation to preserve the life and well-being of the population. Going out into the streets and carrying out their daily tasks turned them into heralds of life, guaranteeing the continuity of basic services and access to goods essential for survival. They embodied an endearing normality, providing a sense of security and stability in times of crisis.

However, this essential activity immersed them in a dark and threatening reality. They became potential carriers of an unknown and highly deadly virus by directly contacting the public. This fact linked them to death and imminent danger, exposing them to constant risk to their health and loved ones. Thus, life and death intertwined in their daily work, causing constant emotional and psychological tension.

Governments' political use of the "essential workers" category also contributed to the constitution of the empty signifier of essential society. By designating and listing essential sectors and jobs, governments were attempting to provide a sense of certainty and control amid the chaos and uncertainty of the pandemic. Labeling certain occupations as "essential" gave them particular importance, and their workers became representative symbols of society's resilience and determination in the face of an unprecedented crisis.

However, this categorization also raised profound questions about equity and social justice. Despite its vital role in maintaining normality, the essential society comprises mainly workers whose working conditions are often precarious and marginalized. Many of these employees belonged to undervalued and poorly paid sectors, which generated tensions over the perception of their actual value and recognition by society and employers.

The essential society during the COVID-19 pandemic acquired a complex and contradictory meaning. It functioned as an empty or floating signifier that symbolized the duality of life and death, normality, and uncertainty. Essential workers became embodiments of bravery and vulnerability, carrying the emotional weight of an entire society's hopes and fears. Its vital role and inclusion in government discourse sought to provide certainty in times of uncertainty but also highlighted existing structural inequalities in society. Essential society was ultimately a mirror of our social history, revealing the complex interconnection between the functioning of society and the working and social conditions of those who sustain it.

THE PARADOX OF THE ESSENTIAL SOCIETY

The emergence of the "essential society" during the COVID-19 pandemic brought a paradoxical and multi-faceted concept to the forefront. This societal construct could be viewed as a double-edged sword, symbolizing hope and a source of ambiguity, reflecting the interplay of life and death, normality, and uncertainty.

The Heroes Among Us

In the eyes of the public, essential workers became modern-day heroes. They donned the mantle of courage and resilience, navigating high-risk scenarios to ensure the survival and well-being of the population. Venturing out into the world during a crisis, they were heralds of life, maintaining the flow of essential services and ensuring access to vital goods. Their dedication provided a semblance of normality, offering security and stability in turbulent times.

The Dark Underbelly

Nevertheless, this heroic narrative existed alongside a darker reality. Essential workers, by their direct contact with the public, became potential carriers of a mysterious and highly lethal virus. Their roles intertwined life and death, exposing them to constant risks to their health and loved ones. The emotional and psychological toll of this constant tension was an unspoken burden they carried as they grappled with their role in society's battle against an invisible enemy.

Governments' Ploy

Governments played a pivotal role in shaping the "essential society." By designating specific sectors and jobs as "essential," they aimed to instill a sense of order and control amid pandemic chaos. This labeling elevated these occupations to positions of particular importance, with the workers becoming symbolic representations of society's resilience and determination in the face of an unprecedented crisis.

The Price of Recognition

However, this categorization also sheds a harsh light on profound equity and social justice questions. Despite their undeniable contribution to maintaining a semblance of normality, the essential society primarily comprised workers whose labor conditions were often precarious and marginalized. Many of these employees toiled in undervalued and underpaid sectors, igniting tensions over the perception of their true worth and the recognition they deserved from society and their employers.

The "essential society" that materialized during the COVID-19 pandemic encapsulated a complex and contradictory narrative. It stood as a vacillating signifier, emblematic of the dualities of life and death, normality and uncertainty. Essential workers straddled the roles of brave heroes and vulnerable individuals, carrying the weight of an entire society's hopes and fears on their shoulders.

Their critical role and their inclusion in government discourse aimed to provide a semblance of certainty amid turbulent times. However, in doing so, it laid bare existing structural inequalities within society. The "essential society" reflected our social history, revealing the intricate interplay between the functioning of society and the working and social conditions of those who sustained it.

ARBEIT MACHT FREI: THE SKETCH OF SOME CONCLUSIONS.

The analysis of the emergence and evolution of the concept of "essential society" has shed light on the complexity and contradictions surrounding this categorization. Although it emerged as a response to the urgency of maintaining the functioning of society during the crisis, the notion of an essential society also revealed profound social and labor inequalities rooted in our economic and political structures.

In the context of the pandemic, essential workers became essential actors but also potential victims of exposure to the virus. Their dedication and bravery in facing high-risk situations earned recognition and gratitude from world leaders. However, this same situation of constant exposure raised questions about the absolute protection and valuation these employees received outside of government rhetoric.

The categorization of essential workers became an empty or floating signifier that brought together in one place the fears and hopes of society during the pandemic. The duality of their work, between life and death, endearing normality, and the imminent end, generated emotional and psychological tensions for both essential workers and society.

The political use of essential society also revealed how specific precarious and marginalized labor sectors were condemned to shoulder the vital responsibility of maintaining the functioning of society. This highlighted the capitalist and hierarchical logic that has permeated our society, where those who uphold the fundamental foundations are often the same ones who suffer from labor and salary inequalities.

Ultimately, the essential society was not created by the pandemic but instead highlighted and made the underlying social structures visible. The exclusion of naked life, sovereign violence, and capitalist logic was manifested during the crisis.

This book has contributed to analyzing the relationship between naked life and politics, exclusion and inclusion, vulnerability, and heroism in the context of the COVID-19 pandemic. While emerging as a response to maintaining normality in times of crisis, the essential society has also laid bare the gaps and challenges in our social and economic structures, urging greater recognition and protection of those who support the backbone of society. Thus, the pandemic has been an opportunity to reevaluate and rethink our approach to essential workers and the inequalities they face in the hopes of building a more just and equitable society in the future.

EPILOGUE

I write in a hurry as if I have a clock behind my back that constantly reminds me that time is moving and that if I don't catch it on paper, it will disappear forever.

I wrote this concise book in a very short time, just a few weeks after the first idea came to me almost as a surprise when I was reading about the exhaustion of the medical sector after the pandemic, especially after listening to nurses and doctors who confessed to me that they were exhausted, that they couldn't handle a new wave or a pandemic similar to Covid-19.

They are so essential that they become dispensable. A perverse logic, but prevailing. Isn't that the commercial logic of capitalism? What you need most is what you should always have a spare part for. For this reason, I apologize if the book does not exhaust or meet the formed initial expectations.

If this is the case, see this book as a provocation.

JUAN M. FERNÁNDEZ CHICO

Nació en la frontera entre México y Estados Unidos un 17 de septiembre de 1985. Estudió un doctorado en ciencia política y abandonó la academia para perseguir otros sueños. Ha escrito varios libros, entre ellos Correspondencias, cartas, figuras y personajes, *junto con Alfonso Herrera,* Excluidos funcionales y subjetividades políticas *y la novela* La isla de los ancianos. *Es productor, guionista y director de cine.*

AFTER THE STORM
EDITORIAL

**The essential society: or when life matters
to what extent it is necessary.**
De Juan M. Fernández Chico
Se terminó de editar en
Noviembre de 2023
Por parte de la editorial
After the Storm Editorial

Edición a cargo de Juan M. Fernández Chico